LINES FROM LIFE

LINES FROM LIFE

*Poetry for Those Whose Own Journey
Follows a Crooked Path*

PETER OVERDUIN

iUniverse, Inc.
Bloomington

Lines from Life
Poetry for Those Whose Own Journey Follows a Crooked Path

iUniverse books may be ordered through booksellers or by contacting:

iUniverse
1663 Liberty Drive
Bloomington, IN 47403
www.iuniverse.com
1-800-Authors (1-800-288-4677)

Cover photograph by Peter Overduin.

ISBN: 978-1-4620-7212-5 (sc)
ISBN: 978-1-4620-7213-2 (ebk)

Printed in the United States of America

iUniverse rev. date: 12/21/2011

I live my life line by line.
Anything more would be too much.

Contents

1

Despair

2

Love Lost

3

Loneliness

4

Regret

5

Hopes and Dreams

6

Reflections

7

Sweet Melancholy

8

Songs from the Soul

9

Friendship

10

Love Found

11

Faith

1

Despair

Some people tell me about life and love they have known that is unbounded, as if it were possible that the universe itself could not contain it. Mostly, I've been more comfortable with black holes . . . There are times when I can't seem to crawl in one deep enough or curl up in a space small or dark enough where I don't know if I can go on living, or even want to, and sometimes wish I didn't.

Across the Desolation

...and brown, charred plains
she came to him
like thunder,
a whisper and
a light.

He, restless,
head bowed down,
face covered
in the charcoal dust,
eyes cast down.
Long since has the horizon
ceased its beckoning.
His feet blistered from the journey
to nowhere.
Darkness lights his path:
unutterable pain
and numbness, not feeling.
Grief incomprehensible,
sorrow his song.
Wisps of shadow
Fleeting, always fleeting.
Dance in the sky
darkened by clouds
of tempest rage.

He stood silent
in the center of his pain:
too tired to die,
too weary to live.
His wretchedness cut him
like a knife,
each day dying more,
living less.
No release from the pain.

No sun in his day,
no moon in his night.

No celestial lights
to caress
or bring life
to the place of desolation
that was his abode:
his heart.
She burst forth then;
what love it was
that dared
break the silence
with laughter,
tears,
and joy!

He groaned in pain,
bones broken by grief,
eyes blinded by
darkness.
He did not see,
and
into this place she came.
She found him there,
broken,
scarred,
ragged,
and blind.
Heart long since silenced
of songs with joy.

His eyes,
like broken windows
to a darkened soul
long lost,
not caring,
not comprehending.

"Lift up your eyes,"
she whispered to him.
"Give me your hand,
and I will lead you."

He sat motionless,
the shattered pieces of his heart
strewn about
the wasteland.
She gathered them in her arms
and bathed them
with her tears.
He moaned, not comprehending.
Trembling,
not believing anymore
in angels,
not remembering.

She knelt there in the dust;
with a gentle hand
lifted up his head.
Her gaze,
a soft, pure light
like beams,
crept into his soul
as the glow
of a single candle
in a darkened room.

With growing wonderment,
he lifted his eyes
to see her who would
kneel there in the dust with him.
Stirrings,
groans,
confusion.

She kissed him there;
his lips
dry, broken, and
cracked.
Her hands upon his cheeks
as she pulled his head
close to hers.
Long, golden
hair shimmered
flowing
in the winds
she brought with her,
blew through
the rooms
and empty corridors
of his heart.
Places long dormant,
lifeless.
Places he had forgotten.

"I will love you,"
she said to him,
"and you will remember
your pain no more."

He awoke then,
prostrate,
in hunger,
still thirsty,
never looking up.
Not able to lift his eyes.
He stumbled
blindly
across the desolation
that was his
loveless,
broken life,
toward the hot

searing sun . . .

"There are no such things
as angels,"
he said.

She cried . . .
as she watched him go.

Looking Back

The year has slipped me by;
suddenly, I feel so much older.
Look around for love,
but I only feel colder.
Oh, that you were near me now,
so I could rest
my weary head upon your shoulder.

The year has gone away;
suddenly, I feel utterly depressed.
There is, it seems, no rest
for this tired mind.
Oh, if I could but hold you now
just for a moment;
I sense you are there,
but I just need to know it.

The year has faded to oblivion;
I feel so insecure
and become so unsure
of thoughts that cross my mind.
It makes me crazy;
I do not know what to do.

This year, as last, leaves me empty.
I ask a lot of questions;
they forever seem to crowd my mind.
I still haven't found the answer
to the ache.

Why? Why? Why?
Each day I die some more inside.
It often gets so intense,
I hide my face in my hands and cry
and fall into bed exhausted.
Even there, sleep and peace elude me;
sighs wrack my weary frame
as I look to the year that is ahead.

Yesterday

Looked at my old letters
then threw them all away.
Gone is the innocence
of yesterday
as I remembered it;
puppy-love notes
on faded yellow papers;
scent of sweet perfumes linger,

so uncomplicated,
so unsophisticated.
Oh, where are all my dreams?
I lost them,
as time and innocence
slipped away,
with every passing
yesterday.

This Road

I cannot go on with games anymore;
even the lies‹ lay broken on the floor.
If love and paradise are somewhere to be found,
why do I live with my face in the ground?

Dreams crash down
my restless, nightmarish sleep.
Visions blur the reality of all I see.
Hope, all but burned out in hopeless failures;
they slowly choke the life out of me.

Once I thought above it I could rise;
now I have trouble just hanging on.
Reality makes lies of all I once held true,
doubting all I once thought I knew.

Once I knew the difference
between fact and fallacy;
now it is all the same to me.
We live in a world where nothing
is right or wrong;
whatever you want, you can believe.

How can I know what to believe in?
When truth is anything,
whatever you want to call it?
Absolute is so passé;
the only thing I know is true today.
Nothing is sure now,
anymore,
in any way.

Questions

Many questions on my mind,
the answers I cannot find.
What are the reasons why?
Do I live only to die?
Does anybody know?
Where does it all go?
Where does it all lead?
What does it all mean?
I do not know what is real;
everything is a mirage,
an illusion to me.
I do not understand what I feel,
and the pain of it all
just never goes away.
I feel it throughout the day.
I wish that I was stronger,
but the nights only get longer,
and the loneliness inside
is something I cannot hide.
What then can I do?
Does the answer lay in you
or
in me?
I cannot see
through the walls
I have built around me.
I have closed myself in.
I have closed myself out.
Now,
there is nowhere
left to go.

Only Contradictions!

Do I live only to die?
Love, only to say goodbye?
Must I look into lonely eyes,
only to see myself and cry?

Must I make it through the long days
only to struggle through the longer nights?
Must I always live my life alone,
never to find the place I can call home?

Why must I find someone,
only to lose someone again?
Will I finally find myself,
only to despise me for what I am?

Must I see first the lies,
before I can know the truth?
Must I feel first the pain,
before I can know true happiness?

My life is a paradox, full of contradictions,
defying all predictions.
Why then do I wonder, "Why?"
when in the mirror I see only empty eyes.

There must be more to living than dying;
more to love than pain.
There must be more to happy than crying.
Oh, when will I live again?

Sometimes

Sometimes,
I feel so low
that I just
do not know
where to go.

Sometimes,
life
is hard on me.
I find it hard
to see
the way ahead.

Sometimes,
when I think of you
and all you do,
I just sigh.

Sometimes,
I just have to
cry;
I don't know why.

Can you help me find a light?
Can you help me in my fight?
Can you give me back my sight?
Can my heart still know delight?

Oh, just sometime,
just one time!
Can I be free?
Can I be me?
Just one more time.
Sometime?

2

Love Lost

I don't get it. If I lose it, was it ever really mine? If it's a game, I've been a perennial loser. I've lost so many times; I'm not even sure how to play anymore. If it's real, I'm even more in the dark. I wish it didn't matter. I wish I didn't care.

Lament of Love

Walking around
in darkness,
groping for
a ray of
sunlight
that
he seems
to see somewhere;
hoping
to feel
things he
used to feel.
Roses in the
garden,
sweet evening breezes,
early morning dew
on his brow.
But,
it all vanished;
it all seemed to disappear
like snow
on a warm spring day.

When I listened,
I heard him cry
of a love that never
knew repose.
Love that never knew him,
arms that never held him,
as he remembered love
the way it was
when he loved
her.

You

I gave you everything
I was,
I am,
I hope to be.

How can I ever give
again,
to someone else,
all I have given you?

If You Let Me Go

If you are going to let me go,
please let me go slowly;
don't leave me suddenly,
all alone.

I can start all over again,
if you let me go slowly.
Don't shut me out suddenly,
in the pouring rain.

Love me still as a friend;
help my broken heart to mend,
so I can love again.
Stay by me, in the winter of my pain.

Oh, if you are going to let our love go,
please let it go slowly.
Don't just let me go
and leave me, suddenly, all alone.

Burning Memories

I feel the burning memories,
of the way things were before,
when you were here beside me.
Now I am all alone.

Your hand was warm upon mine,
your lips were oh, so sweet.
The look in your eyes just charmed me,
to touch your face just thrilled me.

The words you spoke were soft and kind,
your eyes were deep and blue.
We talked of love and beauty,
all the things that we would do

Now it is all a memory,
going up in flames.
I would give all my tomorrows
for just one yesterday.

Making It Without You

My soul aches.
My heart breaks;
            where are you now?
I don't know how
I can make it through
these long, dark nights without you.

I need you now.
How my heart cries out
for you to come here to me.
I want only to be
close to you.
Oh, how I love you!

Now you are gone.
I will hang on
to the memories
of the love you showed me,
all the little things.
The joy you brought into my life.

I cannot say
how I will find my way,
without the part of me
I gave to you.
Thank you for the part
of you that you gave to me—
forever in my heart.

I think about you every day,
walk, talk with you
            (sounds crazy, I know, but anyway . . .).
Hold you in my dreams,
so close to me it will seem
you are there, beside me.

For the One I Need
but Cannot Love

I do not know what to say.
I am so far away
from where I want to be;
the place where I left me.

Through all the confusion,
through all the sorrow
and my illusions,
I can see tomorrow

but it is not clear,
and you are not near.
I wish that it was yesterday,
and that you were here to stay.

I wish that I could love you.
I know it is you I need
but love is strange to me.
It is one place I have never been.

I wish I knew my mind,
but words are hard to find
to tell you just how I feel.
To know what is not, or what is real.

You loved me like no other woman could.
When I was down you understood.
You treated me right, you treated me good.
If I knew how, love you I would.

Through thick or thin,
sickness or health,
richness or poverty,
in life or in death.

In taking or giving,
happy or sad,
love overcomes all,
if it is true love at all.

Love is giving,
love is living.
I wish I could give you
my love and my life.

But I do not know where to start.
Deep inside I am torn apart
between my mind and my heart.
My confusion, I cannot hide,

I need you to know me,
perhaps make me see
that love is not as far
as I think it is from me.

I Thought You Were the One

You were the one
I thought would understand;
oh, why did you leave me alone?!
You were the one
I thought could take my hand
and lead me home.

You were the one
I thought I would hold forever,
but all I hold now are memories.
You were the one
I thought would make it better;
where are you when I need you near me?

I guess I am just too lost
in myself to see the reasons
why love never happens to me.
Maybe it is just the time or just the season,
but ever since you have gone,
I have been so lonely.

You were the one
I thought would fill my empty space,
but here I cry, alone in this place,
thinking you were the one who would
wipe the lonely tears from my face.

Got lots of friends but
they are all too busy to see
the pain I carry around inside of me.
You were the one, I thought.
I thought you would be the one
for me.

I Just Said, "I Love You"

I thought of a million things I wanted to ask you,
a million things I wanted to say.
But I just said, "I love you."

I wanted to tell you all my meanings,
show you everything I have been dreaming.
But I just said, "I love you."

I wanted to hold you in my arms forever,
promise you we would always be together.
But I just said, "I love you."

I wanted to tell you things I've never told anyone before;
I wanted to give you everything I am—and so much more.
But I just said, "I love you."

I wanted to let go, break down and cry,
as I gently kissed the tears in your eyes.
But I just said, "I love you."

I just said, "I love you," and watched you drive away,
got all choked up, and let despair wash over me.
Then I cried, "I love you," turned, and walked away.

My Love for You

I recall back then,
when we were friends;
we watched the sun
sink into the crimson sea.
You and me.

I remember when,
as we lay there in the sand,
a bed of crystals
clinging to you like diamond
sparkles in the evening sky.
You reached out and took my hand
as we lay back, side by side, and
watched God paint his tapestry
just for you and me.
I drew your body close to mine;
you told me that you loved me.
There you were—close to me,
just where you should be—
for all eternity.

The times we weren't together,
the times we were apart;
oh, darling, surely you knew!
I left my heart with you.

When you did not have me to hold,
you just thought of me and felt me near.
When I was not there to kiss your lips,
clutch in desperate embrace;
oh, darling, surely you knew!
I left my heart with you.

Then I threw it all away.
In a single day

I threw my life away.
I am told there are tomorrows
to try and start again,
but I would give them all away
for just one yesterday,
just a day with you
and me.

Oh, I still love you, girl;
your sky-blue eyes
dancing clouds of white
and soft brown hair . . .
I love you, girl!
Your pretty face:
I see it every place and
I want you to know . . .

When you cry and you are lonely,
when you feel you need someone
to hold and stand beside you,
if ever your heart is broken,
remember: I still love you, girl.

If you ever get to thinking
your world has fallen in around you,
and your dreams
all lie in broken pieces on the floor;
when it feels like you cannot go on
living anymore,
remember:
I still love you, girl.

If I could cry out
to have you back!
If I could only shout
to make you see;
you are where I must be!
If I only could—

girl, you know I would.
If I could only understand,
I would make it right, I really would.
I am not sure anymore, what I feel.
I am not sure anymore, what is real.

But each night I think of you,
and I do not know what to do.
I do not know what to do.
To do, oh, what to do.

I do not know what to think;
I am not sure what to say.
Oh, girl! I wish that I could fly away,
just to forget
the love I have for you—
and start again.

My love for you
was a love that tried so hard.
My love yearned always for you.
My love cried.
My love burned.
My love needed.
My love reached out.
My love grew within.
My love for you,

was a love that did not win.
My love was a love that failed
to break the wall
I had put around me.

Girl, this was
my love
—for you.

3

Loneliness

It's that precipice from where I can look over and see the darkness below. I usually let myself fall into that abyss, because it just seems so much easier than trying to find my way back from whatever dark place I am in. It's just easier, sometimes, to be lonely rather than vulnerable. Or rejected. Or to try and only fail. I never "try" to be lonely . . . it just happens that way.

𝓘 𝓐𝓶 𝓐𝓵𝓸𝓷𝓮

When I am with someone else,
I can forget about myself.

When I am alone,
I can only wonder where my life is going.

Though it all seems good for a while,
and on my face I have a smile;

when I am alone,
I wonder where in my hell I am going.

No one wants to be alone;
we all need that place called "home."

We all need to love and to belong;
without that, life just goes routinely on.

We all have our song to sing,
but we are often too afraid to begin

because, inside, aren't we alone?
Don't we wonder where we're going?

I am trying to share myself with you,
but I find it very hard to do

because, inside, I am so empty and alone,
and I just do not know where I am going.

I am alone . . .

Unreached Horizons

Nothing matters anymore.
I lay curled up on the floor;
my time has come.
Do I run?

Each day, every day, forever in my life,
I look with longing at the end of a rope.
I am young but don't feel much hope
for the life ahead of me.

I have drifted most of my years;
my mind is filled with fears.
My eyes weep the tears
of a lonely man; life, so cold and dreary.

I cannot define this loneliness.
I cannot plumb the depth of these dark thoughts.
My heart is filled with hopelessness;
for many years, it is happiness I have sought.

I live life at the end of dead-end roads.
Every new horizon I think I just reached
only taunts me, revealing new horizons that goad
me on to the next path that ends in blackness.

Please Stay

Talking with you
makes me realize
how much I have wanted
to meet someone like you;
someone I can talk to.
Please stay,
a little while longer.

There have been so many changes,
so many realizations
I have only just begun to realize.
It is good for a crying heart
to pour itself out,
so please stay,
a little while longer.

It is hard to keep
what I feel inside.
I am not one to hide.
It is hard to carry it alone,
no one to share my burden.
So please stay,
a little while longer.

A Soldier's Life

I am all alone in the middle of the night,
no one here to hold me.
Cold and damp come morning light,
no one here beside me.

A soldier's life is a lonely one,
so much time away from home.
Sleet and snow, rain, pray for the sun,
always looking for a phone.

Drink and fight and talk a lot,
anything to chase the blues away.
All the time counting down the days
to when I am home to stay.

For me, each day is a lonely day,
because even after a time away,
coming home to an empty place—
oh, that is when I really miss a pretty face.

Well, I travel a lot and know all their names,
but I am sick of playing these games.
One of these days a woman will come along,
and we will play those "forever" love songs.

Got the Blues Again

I wrote some words;
cannot find the ones that fit.

They just fly away like birds.

Thoughts of you crowd my mind,
the words to describe
just how it is I feel
get all jumbled up inside.
You won't be there
when I get back,
so I don't care
if I make it home today.
Without you there,

I will just be lonely anyway.

Oh, how I need to be held by you,
just to know everything's okay.
I have a bad case of the blues,
because

you are so far away.

For me it's always been the same;
she is gone,
all I'm left with are the dreams.
Memories of faded dreams;
always the same old story.

She is gone.

I am tormented by memories.
Please come back and stay with me.
Come back,
do not stay away.

Return to me.

Though I am not sure
of everything I need,
I know I need you now.

I need you.

I do not know if you understand
everything I am trying to say here.
I wish you were here
to wipe away these lonely tears,
to hold me close,
these first few hours of this new year.
Just hold me close,
till morning light draws near.

I Wish

Music pounding in my head,
figures in the dim light
sway to the throbbing beat,
silhouettes in mist
that rises, ebbs and flows,
stabbed by flashes of light;
myriad of lasers
that illuminate
the dance floor.

I stay in my seat.

Smiling faces all around me,
laughter
hauntingly shallow,
out of tune,
like the games of lust
and love
played out, ending,
inevitably, with tears
in drunken misery.

You are all I see.

I do not want to dance,
I have had my chance,
overwhelmed by
a sense of futility
and emptiness.
I look at all the faces;
none of them are you.
They fade into oblivion.
I see only you; you are the only one.

I wish that you were here with me.

Look into My Eyes

I have been working all day;
don't have much to say.
It is quiet here at home;
I am all alone.

I am too alone to smile,
though I do try it every once in a while.
Look into my eyes, and see a trace
of the loneliness
I do not let show on my face.

My heart cries out within me
for a love to show me
a new reality;
the way life should be.

I have never minded being alone
but lately—it's been being lonely
that I find hard to take.
It makes my heart break.

When, sometimes,
I feel I have nothing left to live for,
why does losing something I do not have
make it harder still
to get back the feelings I once had?
Love it was, I know,
but in my eyes it never shows.

Look into my eyes
and see a trace
of the loneliness I do not let show on my face.
Look into my eyes,
and peer into my soul,
for a love that was
but is no longer there.

4

Regret

I wish I took the lifeline you threw me. I wish I didn't take the leap over that perilous edge and free-fall into darkness. I wish I had allowed myself to hope when I saw the Light you shone on my path to show the Way. I wish I didn't just stay right where I was. But I did. And when I did get up and go, it was always in the wrong direction.

It Was I

Oh, how I wish
I could get you out of my head,
think of someone else instead.
But you will not let me be alone,
tossed about on a stormy sea.

Oh, the times
I wish I never met you;
the pain you put me through!
The memories never let go,
and bring me down so low.

The irony of it all,
and this most painful memory
I vividly recall,
always;
it screams as though you were here:

> It was I who left you,
> not wanting you near.

Could There Be Somebody Else?

Could there be someone else?
Part of you,
part of me,
part of both of us?

Could there be somebody else?
Who will watch her grow?
Will she grow up all alone?
Will she have a happy home?

Could there be someone else?
Someone who will never know me?
Someone I will never see;
could it really be?

Could there be someone else?
Will I give up a part of myself,
to never feel the same again?
How can I live with the pain?

Could there be someone else?
Will my soul be held as ransom for her own?
Will I ever gaze into a child's eyes,
and not see part of me—and cry?

Looking at You, Old Man, Looking at Me

I see
regret and agony;
memories
of years gone;
old, faded face
wrinkled with age.
Pain crosses, contorts
the reddened face,
convulsed
with a rasping cough,
spit, and wheezing.
Your eyes
see through drooped eyelids
and are lifeless.
I see me.

I see
the curse of labour;
the broken body
sick with cancer of old age;
feeble hands only able
to grasp that glass of beer,
slowly, shaking, to your lips.
Wisps of smoke curl up
from the dangling cigarette
clenched between yellowed teeth
and hover like halos;
clouds of death
in the thick stench
above you.
I see me.

Where shall I go
from here?
Regretting my years,
everything I wanted to do
but didn't do yesterday.
I just look at you,
old man,
looking at me.
I see me.

What now?
From where shall lost years
be given back to me,
so I can escape the searing pain
of looking at you,
old man,
looking at me.
Lifeless your eyes,
empty and troubled your face.
About what shall we converse?
Glories of your past?
Memories of years gone by?
Years not seen
since many years?
Drink, old man;
drink
to dreams and lost years.

Like you, old man,
I shall become.
Knowing only where I came from,
never where I am going
or finally shall go.
The young?
They will see me then;
old, broken, and lost.
They will see themselves,
as I see me,
old man,
when I see you.

Wishing for Yesterday

Wasted years, a thousand tears,
and I am no farther ahead
than I was before,
when I was way behind.

I look for lost time;
where did it all go?
I do not know
where I am going,
but know where I have been
and wish;
I wish, I wish, I wish
I could go back
to the way I
used to dream,
and play, and love.
I want to start
all over again.

Time is a healer, some say,
but look at me today!
The pain of yesterday
just will not go away.
It will not go away.

5

Hopes and Dreams

I have them, I guess, but I live life in the moment. It helps me forget how many of them died along the way, and unless I wrote them down, I don't even remember what they were.

In a Dream

The flowers bloom;
very soon
the trees will be green.

I lie here by the sea;
tall green grass surrounds me.
I am thinking of you, I am in the dream.

The sun sets low over the hills;
its beautiful color fills
the evening sky.

The waves lap gently on the shore;
the moon has never been so beautiful before.
I am thinking of you.

I dream about you.
I always think about you.
I really love you, you know I do.

I go to sleep with you
on my mind; you are there when I wake up, too.
I think of you, the whole day through.

Never Again

Sometimes I get so frustrated,
wonder if I'll make it.
Depression takes its hold on me.

I weep silently to myself.
I sit
                    alone.

I stare at a tree,
alone but free.
Does it know what I feel?

The breeze cools my tear-stained face.
It's the only friend I have in this place.
Being without you is being alone.

Sadness and sorrow fill my heart;
all I can do tonight
is sit here and try to write.

I must be near you soon;
talk and share love under the stars;
never again will you be so far away.

Never again will I leave you.
Never again will I hurt you.
Always will I love you.

When I Think of You

We have only known each other
a little while.
When I think of you, I smile,
and lose myself as I run free
in the spring-green,
flower-filled meadows I see
when I look into your eyes.

I can understand
you are afraid to trust me;
just place your hand in mine,
and let your fear go.
We all get hurt sometimes,
but we must keep trying.
You cannot find love
when you let go of your dreams.

The hurting, crying,
and the pain;
I have been there
many times before.
When I thought I could not
take it anymore,
I always got up to try again.

I think, and remember
how the moon shone gently;
reflecting the beauty
I saw in your face
the first time I saw you.

Now, I am all alone with my dreams;
it seems they bring you closer to me.
Even cold, winter winds
cannot drive away the warmth
I feel in my heart,
when I think of you.

To an Unknown Love

Though I do not know you,
I know you are there,
somewhere.
Though you will never get
my letter,
just to write this
makes me feel better.
Though I do not possess you,
I hope with each day anew
and pray that I might find you.

I need to love you.
I need to feel my arms around you.
I need to know you.

        I am lost without you.

Though I try hard to find you,
you are always

        somewhere else.

When you do need
someone who needs you,
you know

        I will be there.

You only have to call me;
I will come to you,
no matter where I am.
Yes, I will come to you,
no matter where I am
or where you are.

Dream On

Show a smile when you feel it is there,
it can tell someone you care;
a strange and lonely forlorn face
in a busy, cold, and noisy place.

Everyone looks but no one sees;
everyone has ears but no one hears.
Everyone runs but they go nowhere;
it is up to us who understand to care.

Everywhere I look I see people crying,
letting go of dreams, not believing
in much anymore.
When your dreams die, so does your soul.

Do not let go of what you believe in.
We all feel the pain of broken dreams.
Do not give up, let go, do not give in;
one day your dreams will come true.

Dreams may die and hopes fade away
with each painful passing day,
but dreams forgotten never come true.
Cling tightly to the dreams within you.

Dreams

I have dreamed so many dreams,
it always seemed
I would wake up to a nightmare.

When you came into my life,
my dreams became reality.
I found the sunrise of my soul in you.

All my visions for the future,
all my visions—
they are you.

The many dreams that I have dreamed—
dreams I thought would never come true—
I see them come true in you.

Hope or a Dream

Rays of hope
begin to filter through clouds
that hang low over my heart.
I can see the shore
through lifting mist,
and in the distance
I hear
birds sing.
Sweet echoes of hope
across the water—
heard but unseen—
draw me to their call.
The dew carries
with it the fragrances
of the lush forests
and mangroves
whose reflections shimmer
in the calm sea.

If I find this shore
to be but an island,
I will stop my ship and rest,
cry myself to sleep in the sand.
The sea will know my tears;
I will weep for the mirage
love has become. I will mourn
the mirage that is you.

But if I were to land
and find you there,
hold me in your bosom
and let me cry.
Let me hold you.
Wipe my tears with your hair;
tell me, tell me, tell me,
tell me there will be
no more goodbyes.

Together

Could we be
together
a little longer?
Could we grow
together
a little stronger?

Time like a river flows;
together
we grow
and time, like the wind,
breezes away the past
hurts and pains,
bringing us
together.

Could we grow old
together?
Will I still love you
tomorrow?
Or will time, like the wind,
carry my love away
and find me
together
with another?

Together,
tomorrow.
How lovely it sounds!
Beautiful, the thought,
together
tomorrow
forever.

Life

Your troubled mind:
you cannot seem to find
the answers,
or meaning.
You just keep on dreaming
dreaming, dreaming
your life away,
until one day ...

until one day
you cannot go on any longer.
You fade away
and no one even cares.
No one cares,
because no one knows,
and all this time
you thought you were stronger.
You thought you made it
to where you want to be,
and suddenly you see
you are where you were before.

You know,
it does not
have to be this way.
These words
can be a distant memory
on a better day.
You have got to reach out,
and reach up
to the stars.
They are not that far,
when you really try.

6

Reflections

Sometimes I pause and consider my own existence in the mirror of life as it happens around me. I always manage to see the dark lining to a perfect sunset.

I Thought

Tonight,
as I lay on my bed

       I thought,

many are dead
because they
have no place to sleep.

       I should

be thankful for my room.
Many have just a broom
to sweep
rooms they do not own.

       I bet

if they
had a house or room
they would keep it clean;
cleaner than
many of our cleanest.

       I know

they know
what it is like
to live on a bite
or two a day,
and have no house
to clean each day.

       I weep.

The broom in the corner—
just that one broom—
is all they have
to sweep away
their children's bodies,
outside,
in the rain.

The Child

Standing on South Africa's soil
to see the world around.
I see a mother as she gives birth
to a child that cannot live.

The child cries, but who will hear?
The mother cries along.
Space and time have passed me by;
the child now lies still.

The mother now weeps and sighs,
with a look of grief and of pity.
Then she turned to me and spoke
in a language I did not understand.

Although I did not know her words,
I knew that look so well.
She needed help, I understood,
but what could I do?

I kneel beside the little child
who gives a sigh then moves no more.
The sky turns dark, so bleak, so gray,
for the child has now died.

We Never Touch

Hello there, I say to him.
Hi, he says to me.
Bye, I say to him.
Bye, he says to me.

Then
we are gone

to
our own
little

island

in life,

floating,

occasionally running
close to
someone,
stranger,
alien,
but never,
oh,

never touching.

In Search of Self

In search of self,
discovering
the essence of my being.
Seeking to discern
things I sense,
but cannot see.
Try to discard
pretences,
feelings; real,
though
I do not feel them
as real to me;
so distant.
Thoughts there,
I do not think;
I feel them lurk.
Are they really mine?
I grope,
strive to be honest
with myself
and toward others.
In search of self;
a voyage
which takes its course
through deep waters
of my confusion;
sometimes
through waters
of self-satisfaction
and happiness.
Try to find
a place of anchor;
try to find
the place
or time,

where I can find myself.
I ask not for
a world of wealth,
or skill and knowledge;
only
for revelation
of self.
In search of self,
wanting to know
that I may be able
to help many
who are lost
on their own voyage
in search of self.
Am I alone?
Or is there a lighthouse
somewhere
in this ocean of life
where I might find
myself?
In search for self,
and yet
blown about by
circumstances
and conditions
over which I
have no control.
Yet,
like ships on the sea,
I have a rudder;
but alas!
What use is a rudder,
when I
hail for that shore
which I know not?
In search for the essence of my being.
In search for the truth about myself.
In search for self.

Wild and Free

Wild and free
just like the sea
　　　　you and me

our spirits reach high
like the mountains
into the sky
　　　　sometimes I cry

when I look deep
into your eyes
I see the sun
　　　　in a calm lake mirrored
　　　　and the mind

of one who
knows
　　　　the freedom of the sea

one who understands
me

　　　　wild and free

Walk in Shadows

You cannot find love
in the darkness.
Though shadows
follow in the light,
it is better to
walk with the shadows
than to
walk alone in the night.

The Glassy Sea

White clouds
against a blue sky
reflect on algae green water
lapping at my sides.
I wonder
how this has never changed,
when I have.

Bright lights
against a dark sky;
silver sands cool
beneath my feet.
I wonder
how this has never changed,
when I have.

Vibrant life,
montage of the sea,
uncaring and free
all around me.
I wonder
how this never changes,
when I have.

Where is the love?
Infinite,
forever it grows,
wider than the universe,
deeper than the sea,
brighter than the sun,
and the stars of the night sky!

Oh! how is it
that I have changed?
When all this
has remained the same,
how all this
has always been the same.

Do you sense my longing,
forever unfulfilled?
Can you feel my hunger?
The cry of my soul?
The passion, always fleeting,
forever burns.

My love is like
winds that blow:
sometimes a gentle breeze,
sometimes a terrifying howl.
Why is it so often
not felt at all?

My love is like
ocean waves that lap the shore:
sometimes a gentle caress,
sometimes a raging storm.
But ever the glassy sea
hides all that is within me.

What If . . .?

Deep brown eyes
against a blue sky;
trees towering overhead,
swaying to and fro
in the gentle sweeping breeze
that caresses us;
intertwined
on a bed of moss,
on the shores
of a lapping sea.

What if . . . I loved you?

Sweet,
soft skin;
gentle touch,
tenderness, affection,
patient and lovely.
Lips so full,
luscious,
touching;
fingers dancing
on my skin,
caressing,
embracing,
and forgetting.

What if . . . you loved me?

Minds speak
where mouths
make no sound.
Heart melting
at your smile.
I yearn for you,
miss you,
listen for your voice.
Eyes like windows
to a deep place
where I am lost,
never wanting
to be found.

What if . . . I loved you?

Sweet glances;
I can tell
you want to touch me.
Feel my touch,
my hands upon you,
clutching you
in sweet embrace.
Our lips meet,
eyes wide open, staring
arms around each other,
consumed in our lust.

What if . . . we loved each other?

If I loved you,
would I yearn more
for you?
Crave more? Your touch?

Would the fire
burn brighter still?
Would my heart
beat faster yet
at your sweet words?

Would my thoughts soar
higher than
the eagle's wings?
Would my words flow
from yet deeper
places?
Would my flesh
be yet more fulfilled
with your giving?

If you loved me,
would you tell me
that you missed me more?
Would you share
more words with me,
laying your soul bare
for me to touch?
Would your loving
be more beautiful yet?
Would my touch
excite you more?

What if . . . we loved each other?

7

Sweet Melancholy

There have been those rare times when my spirit soars; when people or places bring out a lofty disposition in me I didn't know I had. Indeed, how sweet those moments are; how sad to see them slip away. But they do.

If You Could See Me Now

I have always missed you
in some way;
thinking of you,
day to day.

Friends gone, yet not forgotten;
memory of your soft touch lingers on,
kisses sweet,
morning forest mist.

Why would you think of me now?
What is it you think
you see,
in your memory of me?

What would you think of me now?
Would you still care for the man
you thought was—
but is not—what you thought he might be?

Oh!
That I could be with you tonight,
lying next to you
in shades of candlelight,
loving you in
shadows of night.

You Make Me Happy

It feels so good to hear you speak
about the way you feel.
I have not heard anyone talk
like you in a long, long time.

You read my writing, and you read it well;
you know just what I tried to say.
More than what I have written there,
I have a heart of overflowing yet to tell.

Oh! You make me feel so good,
and I would like to ask you if you could
just hold me one more time,
make me feel the way I never thought I would.

It is so good to get to know your mind;
beautiful thoughts there I find.
Makes me want
to get to know you better.

Don't you go away,
don't you ask me to go away;
right now,
right here beside you
is where I want to stay.

Hold you close to me;
so close to me.
You make me happy,
oh, lady,
you make me happy!

I Will Love You

I will miss you
when you're gone;
no one to hold me
when nights are long
and lonely.

I will miss the lips
that kissed me
in the morning before the dawn.
I long already for arms to hold me;
I feel so lonely.

Oh, to feel again
your firm embrace!
Need it now, in this empty place.
I reach out for you
but I find you not.

I wonder when
I might know again
the traces of your fingers
soft upon my skin;
light as the morning dew
sparkling on the grass
every day anew.

If you are to be
mine forever,
I will give to you
my love, forever.

If you are but to be
the one meant,
the one sent for me to see
that I can love for the first time,
then still I would love you,
for all time.

From Me to You

Sometimes I wonder
what I am doing here.
I am not without my fears,
not without my tears.

I often think of you.
I wonder what you do
while I am far from you,
so many miles away.

At night I kiss your picture.
I know for sure
I love you.
I hope you love me too.

At night I lay thinking
about the times we have together.
I feel my spirit sink
because I cannot be with you.

Words Can Never

I cannot express myself.
Words will never tell how I feel about you;
words will never do.

I cannot say what is on my mind.
It's way too much and I cannot find
words to express myself.

Your smiling face and gentle touch;
you are too much
for words.

I hold you in my mind;
again, I cannot find
the words to describe it.

When I look into your eyes,
I begin to cry.
Words could not explain why.

Words could not explain the feeling
I feel when you kiss me.
Words could never say the visions that I see.

Words could never
say how much I love you.
Words could never
say how much I need you.
But words are all I have
to tell you that I do.

Watching Over You

Soft shades of misty moon
shining down into your room,
where you lie dreaming;
I am watching over you.

How quietly you sleep!
Moonbeams caress you as they creep
around you like silent angels;
I am watching over you.

I bend down to kiss your lips
and whisper softly in your ear.
You moan softly; do you hear the words,
"I am watching over you"?

What do you dream of now?
I wish that I could read your mind,
and I wonder what thoughts there I would find
as I watch over you.

You lie sleeping there so sweetly;
would you dream a little dream of me?
In your dreams before the dawn,
can you see me there, watching over you?

Morning slowly breathes new light across the sky.
You awake and rub your sleepy, dreamy eyes,
wondering what the day will bring for you.
Know that I am watching over you.

Isn't It Beautiful?

Isn't it beautiful?
The way we can speak
words
to each other,
and not make a sound?
My heart is full
of words for you.
Isn't it beautiful?
The way we can look
into each other's eyes,
and understand why
we love each other?
It makes me cry.
Isn't it beautiful?
The language of our minds
is only love, and often
I cannot find
words to tell you,
how much I love you.
And I do love you;
I truly do
love you.
In the silence of our love
that we feel toward each other
when we are together,
watching the sun set
low over the hills,
my heart is filled
with just one thought
and a million words:
I love you.

Too Soon to Love, Too Late to End Love Now

You fill my dreams in sleepless nights.
I toss and turn, but try as I might,
I find no rest for my tortured soul
and wish only for the morning light.

You came into my life at a time
when everything was going fine.
Love was the last thing I wanted to find,
meant for another place, another time.

But now you are here, and what shall I do?
I just can't get you out of my mind.
I just cannot run from myself anymore.
I fall, broken, to the floor.

How shall I feel, what shall I say?
I think about you every day,
and here I am now, so far away
from your embrace, where forever I want to stay.

You look at me with penetrating eyes,
and what you tell me now, it makes me cry;
then you laugh at me and I laugh along,
because it is you doing this to me.

But oh! for the heart to really know;
just how much can I let my feelings go?
I am so afraid there will come the day,
you will take your love away.

But, until then, I cannot just stop and go back in time,
though I've tried, and now it's more than friends.
In my heart, there are thoughts I find
telling me that this time, I do not want it to end.

Will You Lie with Me Here?

Will you lie with me?
On the shores of a stormy sea,
let me love you.
Will I know your touch?
Mighty waves
crash on the shore,
sending out their awesome roar;
your soft whisper is all I hear.
In the bright, warm afternoon sun,
ocean sprays make rainbows
dance in their joy.
Mist glistens on your soft skin,
and I wonder:
Will you lie with me here?
Will you let me love you?

Again Tonight

Again tonight,
I am alone;
wish I was home
with you.
I feel lonely, need you:
somewhere
to rest my weary soul.

Again tonight,
I think of you,
looking at your picture on my wall,
and just hope you will call.
I feel a little low;
home is where I want to go.
I want you to know
home is you.

Again tonight,
I want you to know
I really miss you.
I wish that I was with you now.
I need you
to help me through
the darkness of my night.

Again tonight,
words cannot say just how I feel.
They are feelings words just can't make real,
and in those quiet moments here alone,
my thoughts and feelings are with you.

Again tonight,
this I want you to know:
my thoughts of you
will go on and on.

Cry, Lady, Cry

I see you in those lonely faces,
I see you in those lonely places
where broken hearts—they hide
behind crying eyes. Lady, I see you.
I am trying to get through to you.
Cry, cry, cry,
oh lady, cry,
because no matter what they say,
crying washes the pain away.
Don't you know
the sun won't shine
until after the rain?
Cry, cry, cry,
oh lady, cry.
Crying is for those who try,
hurting, for those who care.
Lady, I know, and I've been there
so many times before,
when I lay alone,
cold and shivering on a frozen floor;
it hurt less than a lonely bed.
Cry, cry, cry,
oh lady, cry.
A stone-cold heart, it never breaks,
but lady, you've got what it takes
to give more love
than any man could ever need.
Don't you throw it all away,
because there will come that day
when I will not have to say,
cry, cry, cry,
oh lady, cry.

8

Songs from the Soul

Some things can only be sung. Mere words are not enough. I sometimes think the music that wells up in me is but another place for me to hide from my sadness and escape from the darkness.

Come to Me

I feel so confused,
my mind feels so abused;
I don't know what I am thinking
and feel my spirit sinking.

You ask me if I love you,
I don't know what to tell you;
I know what I believe
but don't know what to feel.

> Come to me, oh, come to me,
> take me in your arms and comfort me.
> Love me, babe, oh baby, please love me,
> 'cause right now I feel so lonely.

Maybe it's just that I don't know you
as well as I would like to;
Maybe it's just that you're so far away.
Oh, I fight this battle every day.

Maybe it's just that I don't understand myself;
this is where I need your help.
Maybe it's just that I don't know what I need;
don't know where my life's road is leading.

> Come to me, oh, come to me,
> take me in your arms and comfort me.
> Love me, babe, oh baby, please love me,
> 'cause right now I feel so lonely.

Oh, I have a heart full of emotions,
but they're all in one big commotion,
and you're not here; to get to know you better,
all I can do is write you a letter.

If this is love, well, I don't understand it;
feel so lost now, and I just can't stand it.
where are you, oh, I need you now;
I need to love you, but don't know how.

      Come to me, oh, come to me,
      take me in your arms and comfort me.
      Love me, babe, oh baby, please love me,
      'cause right now I feel so lonely.

I Need Someone

I don't know what to say;
I think about you every day.
I know you are sad I am going away.
What can I say?

I sit here and stare across the water;
everything in nature all fits in so nicely.
I wonder if,
maybe someday,
we will be that way.

The water is free,
and I feel so free,
yet I know I need someone.

The wind rushes by;
it needs no one
to tell it where to fly.

I've been like the wind,
going where I want to,
but now I know

I need someone.

It's Not Easy to Say Goodbye

It's not easy to say goodbye;
I know it makes you cry.
I understand why.
Please don't feel like you want to die.

I'm sorry for the way I treated you.
I'm sorry I cannot be what you want me to be.
I'm sorry you find it hard to understand.
I'm sorry I cannot give a helping hand.

Please do not think there is nothing left to live for;
your heart is young and free.
I know right now you do not see it;
someday you will understand.

I know it hurts you that I am leaving;
I wish I knew what to say.
Just do not spend your young years grieving
about a love that never came your way.

I know that it's not easy to say goodbye.
I know it makes you cry.
I understand why;
please don't feel you want to die.

It's not easy to say goodbye.

My Dreams Died in Reality

I once had a lot of dreams
about how I would love you.
I swore that I could never,
that I could never let you down.

When I thought about a family,
I could just see me
loving our children faithfully,
like no one loved before.

> Oh, but it seems
> my dreams died in reality;
> the reality of me.
> Oh, please forgive me.

I saw me help you every time
you were a little tired.
I saw my smile come through
every time you were a little blue.

I saw myself as someone strong,
someone you could look up to.
I dreamt that I would never fall;
I would always be there when you called.

> Oh, but it seems
> my dreams died in reality;
> the reality of me.
> Oh, please forgive me.

Though I knew times could be rough,
it didn't worry me 'cause I thought I was tough,
and nothing could get in the way
of me loving you perfectly every day.

Over time, my dreams slowly die;
I see them slip away.
I wonder why, with each new day,
you stay and love me.

> Oh, but it seems
> my dreams died in reality;
> the reality of me.
> Oh, please forgive me.

When You Need Me

Are you lonely tonight?
You cannot find the light?
Stay here by my side;
together we will fight.

Do the tears begin to fall?
Just begin to call.
I will be there by your side;
I will help you through the night.

Is your load too much to bear?
You know I will be there.
You know I really care;
there is no need to be scared.

I have seen you through and through;
I want you to know I love you.
You know I want to help you.
I want to help you start anew.

Just a Man

(for Orville)

He's a man who would give you his time;
he's a man who would be your friend.
He'll walk with you and help you find
your way; he'll walk with you to the end.

He's a shepherd who cares for his sheep;
you will find him there when your way is steep.
I never heard him close his door
to anyone looking for more.

> And he's just a man
> doing what he can,
> and we love him.

He's a man never short of a smile,
and he'll sit and talk with you awhile.
At times when I feel a little colder,
he's there with his arm around my shoulder.

He's a man who will love you like a brother;
you'll always find him doing something for another.
He's a man with a lot of emotion,
and he's got love as big as the ocean.

> But he's just a man
> doing what he can,
> and we love him.

> Yes, you're just a man
> doing what you can,
> and we love you.

I Understand

How can I make you see
your life is worth living to me?
How can I make you care
for yourself? When you need me,
I'll be there.

When you feel you're all alone,
when you're running, and you have no home,
I want you to understand
I'll be there, to give a hand.

There's no reason to give up,
but if you feel like crying,
I'll understand,
because I've cried myself before.

When you wake up in the middle of the night
and you find yourself praying for daylight,
because you're all alone, and this isn't your home,
I want you to know, yes, I want you to know . . .
there's no reason to give up.

But when you feel like crying,
let me hold your trembling body close to mine.
Let me look into your eyes and tell you
that I understand.

When I Walked Out on You

What have I done?
What did I do
when I walked out on you?

In leaving you I left behind
the better part of me.
No one ever got so close to me
as you got to me.
No one ever needed me
the way you needed me.
And I know I never needed anyone
the way I needed you.
You were all I needed in someone else,
but I am not what I should be myself.

What have I done?
What did do
when I walked out on you?

Please understand,
it is not that I don't love you.
But I just could not see
the vision that you tried to offer me.
I know that if our love is meant to be
it will happen again,
but until then . . .

Don't Be Afraid of the Night-time

No, it's not that you aren't beautiful;
it's not that I don't want you.
It's because you are a lost and lonely girl;
you don't know what you want or what to do.

Any man would fall when you look into his eyes;
any man would melt at the touch of your hand.
But your love comes from a lonely, broken heart,
and lonely, broken love is no love at all.

> Oh baby, don't be afraid of the night-time,
> 'cause morning has to come sometime.
> When you look back and face the you
> you've come from,
> you will grow into the you
> you always wanted to become.

Beaten, lied to, never-ending abuse;
made bitter and angry, left lonely and confused.
Night-time brought terror, now you're afraid of the dark;
trapped in despair, you just tear yourself apart.

What they did to you was a hideous wrong.
Life so broken, discarded, its givers departed.
Your young heart hardened, told what a loser you are;
the soul just fell to believing they were right all along.

> Oh baby, don't be afraid of the night-time,
> 'cause morning has to come sometime.
> When you look back and face the you
> you've come from,
> you will grow into the you
> you always wanted to become.

You've got to get yourself together,
try to start again.
I know sometimes the sun won't shine,
but you will learn to ride out stormy weather.

You can't run away from what has been,
but you can change what is to come.
It isn't going to get any better than what you've seen
unless you try to change some.

> Oh baby, don't be afraid of the night-time,
> 'cause morning has to come sometime.
> When you look back and face the you
> you've come from,
> you will grow into the you
> you always wanted to become.

I Won't Let You Go

I never met a woman who loved so deeply,
but your tears are blinding your eyes
to the love that I have for you.
Oh, why don't you let your tears go?

I'll give you my heart—it's right here for you!
But you won't take it, 'cause you're hanging on
to your pain with both hands.
Oh babe, why don't you let your pain go?

> Oh, baby! Why don't you just let it all go?
> Come running to me and I'll tell you,
> as I'm holding you tight, oh, how I love you so!
> Oh, baby, just let it all go—I won't let you go!

You push me away; you want me to stay;
you won't take what I am trying to give you.
Baby, I've got to know!
Why won't you let me break those walls down?

The hardest thing is not talking to you,
not hearing from you, hoping you work it all through.
The things I've said and done—baby, you know!
Oh, why don't you let your fears go?

> Oh. baby! Why don't you just let it all go?
> Come running to me and I'll tell you,
> as I'm holding you tight, oh. how I love you so!
> Oh. baby, just let it all go—I won't let you go!

I don't know if you even heard;
did you even listen to my words?
Couldn't you hear through your hurt and your pain?
Oh, babe, why don't you let your hurt go?

I can't take your pain, baby, you've got to give it to me!
My heart is open, just look up and see.
I'm waiting for you with arms wide apart, oh ...
Oh babe, why don't you just let it all go?

      Oh, baby! Why don't you just let it all go?
      Come running to me and I'll tell you,
      as I'm holding you tight, oh how I love you so!
      Oh, baby, just let it all go—I won't let you go!

Bad Days, Sad Ways

You said there would be bad days;
you wondered if I'd go away.
I said I knew there would be sadness,
but I'd do more than stay.

I know your heart's been broken;
you have heard the words so often spoken,
a thousand times! He would never leave you,
but you awake to find yourself alone.

"Trust" is a word, but how is it earned?
How do you give a heart that's been so often burned?
So, baby, I won't ask you to believe me;
you have heard it all, so many times before.

Oh baby, just give me your bad days!
Drown me in the river of your tears.
Let me lose myself in the valley of your sad ways,
and sink in the dark of your fears.

When the sun will finally shine,
there in your aloneness, my strong embrace you'll find.
My lips, they'll kiss your tear-stained face.
Are you surprised to find me here, in your darkest place?

So I will not say a thing, but you will know
how much I care, when you find me there.
You will feel yourself wrapped in my arms,
where I will keep you from all harm.

Why Can We Not Let Go?

I cannot forget the whispers,
cannot forget your tears
as you lay your head on my shoulder
and told me of your fears.

You would never find a love like ours again,
you said; you cannot let it go,
though I caused you nothing but pain,
more than I will ever know.

> Oh, why can we not move on?
> Why can we not let go,
> when we both know
> we will never be together.

You want to walk away from me;
you wish you just could let it be.
But you don't know how you could move on;
no matter what, it all just feels so wrong.

Oh, I know I will never forget
all the times together since we met.
The love burned hot, even when the pain ran deep.
The world never mattered when we slept.

> Oh, why can we not move on?
> Why can we not let go,
> when we both know
> we will never be together.

Where did it all go? Well, I do not know,
because I live my life one day at a time,
and I never think about the future.
I am always living my life looking behind.

I never think of the pain I cause.
My selfishness; it never gives me pause
to think about what I did to you;
though knowing your love for me was true.

Oh, why can we not move on?
Why can we not let go,
when we both know
we will never be together.

The Lord's Prayer (Revised)

Well, here I am, my Father,
I'm so happy to talk with you this way
and I'm looking forward to heaven ...
Hey! What time is it anyway?

> Oh, Jesus, you know I would do more;
> there's just so little time for ...
> bills to pay, more on the way,
> and my family hasn't seen me yet today.

Ooh, I can't wait to see your kingdom
and to see your will be done
on earth as it is in heaven, Lord;
well, it's late, so I'll just be on my way.

Yes, give me my bread, Lord, but please give me a lot;
I'm always so hungry by twelve o'clock.
Places to go and people to see;
I'm so busy, Lord, don't you see.

> Oh, Jesus, you know I would do more;
> there's just so little time for ...
> bills to pay, more on the way,
> and my family hasn't seen me yet today.

Jesus, you know I hate temptation,
but what is wrong with my television?
I can't just give up my associations.
Don't you want me to witness for you?

The power and glory are yours, Lord;
but God, can I have some too?
'cause if people can't see how successful I am,
Lord, how will they ever believe?

Oh, Jesus, you know I would do more;
there's just so little time for . . .
bills to pay, more on the way,
and my family hasn't seen me yet today.

9

Friendship

The ones that stayed were the ones that really wanted to. I've lost many along the way, some by neglect, but I remember special times: the hurts, pains, laughs, tears, the places we went. Time seems to have brought many more of them out of focus. Like wisps of mist that disappear in the wind. How do you catch them when they are gone?

I Am Your Friend

Sometimes,
life is so confusing
but it will work out in the end.
If you need someone talk to,
come to me; I am your friend.

Sometimes,
love is a pile of broken dreams,
and there are times it seems
all you get from love
are burned-out memories.
I am your friend, lean on me.

Sometimes,
your eyes fill with tears,
you want to cry out your fears,
but there is no one there to hear.
Cry out for me,
I am your friend,
and I am near.

I am your friend
when nights are dark,
long, and lonely.
When none around you
seem to care,
I am your friend.
Reach out for me;
I will be there.

How Can I Ever?

How can I ever thank you?
You have done so much for me!
How can I make you see
just how much I appreciate you?

It is in my leaning on you
that I feel stronger.
It is in loving you
that I get strength to go on yonder.

How can I ever thank you?
I just cannot find the words
to express the way I feel,
the way I feel about you.

I know you do not need me
the way I need you.
I know that you don't care for me
the way I care for you.

How can I ever tell you, anyway,
the meaning of your friendship?
I cannot even grasp it,
what it means to me.

If, One Day

You said some things I needed to hear;
thoughts not heard spoken in so long.
I am so glad to have you near;
a sensitive heart is a beautiful song.

I suppose that most would think
you do not stand out in a crowd,
but the very first time I met you,
I knew I wanted to get to know you better.

It can be a cold and lonely world;
sometimes there is not much to smile about.
Being with you is one of those good times
of sharing, giving—and good things are hard to find.

Would you be my friend?
Will you take from me
all I want to give you?
Me, what I am, all I have, I give to you.

I do not want any more than what you want to give.
I have my life, and you have your own life to live.
But if, one day, our hearts should touch,
let us not let that moment go.

For a Lady, For a Friend

In your dark brown eyes I saw sadness;
it was plain for me to see.
It took just one caring glance from me to know
the feelings you try hard not to show.

Eyes can fight back the tears,
but they cannot hide the fears
mirrored by your broken heart,
nor the hurt that rips you apart.

I know I acted kind of crazy;
it was just my way to make you smile.
I wanted you to see
you could find someone who cares, in me.

Trust betrayed and the promise of love broken—
it is not easy for any one of us to bear.
Come to me, and cry those tears on my shoulder;
I will keep you warm when nights seem colder.

So lay yourself here down beside me,
beneath the night-time star-lit skies
where the water laps against the shore,
and let me help you find yourself once more.

Take It Easy, Think of Me

I know you are not sure
what to think of me,
much the same way
I am not sure about you.

Why don't we just take it easy,
instead of pushing our way through.
The love we yearn for will not come easy;
let's take time for us, you and me.

I need to know the way you feel;
for both of us, broken hearts need to heal.
So hold me close and treat my heart tenderly;
I will draw you close to me and kiss you gently.

When you doubt, are not sure about it,
come to me, we will talk our way through it.
When you feel lonely like nobody cares,
think of me; you know I will be there.

Do not be afraid, you know I understand;
I will come to you when you are sleeping,
come to you in dreams and hold your hand,
stay by your side till dawn creeps in.

Though I fade away as you awaken,
I am by your side throughout the day.
So don't you worry, don't be mistaken;
I will always be there with you, I will never go away.

If You Take Me

Maybe I make you feel a bit uneasy,
but you see,
it's always been that way for me.
Meet someone,
knowing you have to leave,
someone you can talk with,
but you have to leave her be.

Coming back to the place
of childhood ways,
felt like I'd lived here just yesterday,
then you came along, and
suddenly I realized
I'd grown a few years older;
I just look at you and sigh.

Winds of time have blown
across the landscape of my life;
sometimes life is good,
sometimes it cuts deeper than a knife.
I wonder, as I see you sitting there,
if they have left your soul innocent
or left you bare.

Just a little while now; I must go,
return to a place where I can be forgotten.
But if you take me as a friend, as I take you,
who really knows where this will end.
Believe, though I will soon be leaving,
you brought a little light
into this lonely man's being.

You

You are my sister,
you are my friend.
You are an example to me
of who I want to be.
You are a helper
in my time of trouble.
You are there when I need you;
you stay up at night to listen.
You are a river of happiness
that flows into me;
you understand me when I cry.

Now you ask me why I care;
you ask why I'm concerned.
Let me hold your hand;
look at me while I tell you now:
It is because of these I care!
Let me look into your eyes and tell you
it is because you've done so much for me!

It is because of this
and so much more,
why I care so much for you.

You're Beautiful (Just Being You)

High above the snowy clouds
I can almost touch the sun,
but I wish I was homeward bound.

The bright, white clouds and cold, blue sky
are so beautiful, yes, they are so beautiful.
They remind me of you.

It was leaving you
that I found hard to do,
so I wrote these words for you.

When sometime
I come back again,
I know we will still be friends.

All the while I am away from you,
I will hold you in my mind;
you are beautiful, yes, you are so beautiful.

Do not let others change you;
don't do the things they do,
because you are so beautiful—just being you.

You have a smile so beautifully free,
and when you smile that way at me
it is good to know you are someone who cares.

The kindness I see in your eyes
just made it harder to say goodbye;
they are beautiful, yes, they are so beautiful.

You are so beautiful—just being you.

I Have Always Known

I have seen your dreams
cry a thousand tears,
as you watched them slip away.
But I always knew this day would come.

I have felt your pain
through the driving rain;
you thought it would always be this way.
But I always knew this day would come.

I have known the depths of your despair,
when all you saw was darkness everywhere;
you thought that everyone had turned away.
But I have always known I would see this day.

I talked with you through darkest nights,
when your heart was full of fear.
I said it then, and I will say it again,
I have always known I would see this day!

10

Love Found

Somewhere on that crooked, narrow path that leads from despair to faith, love found me.

The Flower

There is a flower
in my heart,
where it has been
many long years.

    I watered it
        with a river of lonely tears
           until the moment
              I met you.

Then I knew:
the flower in my heart
grew there,
to be picked by you.

My Heart, My Heart, Let Go, My Heart!

Not too beautiful—would make her seem unreal—
but pretty; you feel so good to be with her.
Not so forward as to make you afraid;
your singular desire is be to be with her.

She does not talk too often;
you savour the sound of her silence.
Her eyes speak a language
only a heart can understand.

She is a woman and so much a lady;
her laugh brings out the child you see.
Makes you feel a little crazy,
like the first time you fall in love.

She will never hold on to you too tight,
never let you go if you treat her right.
She wants to be close to you and part of your life;
she will give you freedom to be just who you are.

She will tell you her fears and give you her tears;
cry out her torments as you hold her near.
You will know her deepest secrets;
she will trust you with her soul.

She sees the darkness, the anguish in your soul;
she will caress you with her eyes
till you break down and cry;
then draw you to herself and take you high.

A woman, a girl, a lady, and a friend;
she will love you forever if you never let her go.
She will stand by you, see things to the end;
so, my heart, love her, need her, and let your fear go.

When

When I look toward the sunset,
I see your face in the golden skies.
When I wake up to the sunrise,
I see your sparkling eyes.

When I lie awake at night,
I look up at the stars;
I know our love could reach so far beyond,
through what can't be seen ... into Orion's light.

When I see the sun at noonday,
I am even more convinced
our love will burn the brighter;
Its warmth will melt our hearts ... together.

When your tender lips meet mine
and I wrap my arms around you,
I realize then how much I need you,
how much you really mean to me.

And you really mean so much to me.

A Fantasy

Your windswept hair
brushed lightly across my face;
pale shades of cloud-covered moon
danced in the evening breeze.
Soft reflections of faded light
caressed your face,
leaving just a trace
of silver mist upon
your glistening skin.

I gazed into your
eyes and saw there
emotion,
flowing like a river through you.
As I stared I was swept away
in a wild fantasy,
plunging wildly, ecstatically
from one mystical abyss into another,
and finally found my soul
afloat on the fathomless sea of your love.

There I thought my vision perished,
for I slept.
But when I awoke
you were still there.
Searching once again,
deep into your eyes,
I knew then
it had not been
a dream,
and I was lost
forever.

Never Get Used to Saying "I Love You"

I never get used to
saying, "I love you,"
though I think about it
so many times a day.
Such a privilege,
so undeserving;
with each new day I learn
how much you mean to me.

I feel so unworthy
of how you give yourself for me.
I would give my soul for you.

Life is one experience
I would not want to go through
with anyone but you.
I thought the words
would flow so easy,
so easy, so easy;
but I never get used to
saying, "I love you."

A Song in the Night

Even in times like this,
when the pain of the past
causes a tear to glisten;
I know I must listen
to the voice within me
that beckons me on.

Let the past be,
go forward with a song
in your heart!
Though it all may seem so wrong,
give it time,
you will see the light,
and things will turn out right.
Do not be afraid
to love and to be loved.
Love opens many doors
and lets your spirit soar.

Love sets me free
from what is not me
and lets me be me.
Even in the deep of night,
when nary a moonbeam is in sight,
I hear within my heart
the singing of a nightingale.
She brings a song
in my darkest night,
and the darkness around me
becomes my closest friend.
For it is in the darkest times

I think more of you,
and I find,
like the singing
of a bird in the night,
thoughts of you
turn my darkness into light.

A Girl's Last Birthday

She looked back at the early years—
all her hopes,
dreams, and fears—
and never really understood
how, one birthday,
it would be her last.

Now that day has come.
All that went before it
truly lay in the past.
The childhood gifts
and fancies,
all the toys she used to play with,
the friends she knew
and since outgrew;
from today it all is new.

The love that she now shared
just did not compare.
Suddenly, she realized,
she had her greatest gift,
in knowing he would always be there.
None of the presents
she had so joyously opened—
and still made her smile inside
when she thought of them—
could ever take the place
of the gift she'd finally found
in the love he gave her,
and the care she saw there.

She knew
it was her last birthday
as a girl,
and every day from now
was a new birthday,
as a woman.

Love of the Divine

Amazed
at the thought,
prostrate on the ground I fall
at the mere contemplation
that you would love such as me!
—mere mortal, mere man—
That such love
would be bestowed
so giving, selfless, and free
upon me!
Touch of the divine
I can only see,
though, blindly.
How could I comprehend
how you have affected me?

Such beauty!
How indescribable,
indefinable.
That I should lift my eyes
to see,
and weep that you
would look upon me!

My heart bursting forth,
eyes are filled with tears
from weeping.
My soul pained
as though it were ripped
away from me,
longing for your touch.
Fading then
in sheer despair;
I know
such love could ne'er

be mine.
Darkness overwhelms me.

My head shaking back and forth
in grief,
fists slamming down
then raging in the air;
the universe
so dark and cold;
it will not listen!
I collapse,
fall broken to the ground
and fold myself tight.
Oh! that death would release me
from my pain!

Awakened from my stupor
I stir,
my eyes red with tears,
heart rent
from sorrow.
My soul despondent
that tomorrow
would bring relief.

Suddenly,
to my tear-sunken eyes
light appears ...
"Curse the universe!"
I cry,
that it would play
such treachery with me!
But lo ...!
The light grows brighter
as it nears the place
where I lie
feeble, prostrate, broken.
My head sinks low

once more.
Surely the light
is meant for someone else,
not me!
Light of the divine,
once again
to fall upon another?

I feel it then,
in that space I am
so normally in darkness
and cold.
Light so warm,
so bright
and luminescent!
I dare not lift my eyes,
so forgotten, have I,
that light existed
at all;
I tremble
at the sight of it.

The soft, warm glow
of its brightness
envelops me;
I feel so strange
in its presence.
In place of the
tear-soaked ground
around me,
blossoms suddenly appear!
Bright flowers all around!
Their fragrance fills
the air;
my rent heart inexplicably
beating once again
with life!
My soul,

long dark and dormant;
I feel new joy is flowing!
So strange this all
is to me.
Just then,
most wondrous of all,
the Light!
It speaks to me,
such melodious voice,
as if a thousand angels
all broke out
in simultaneous chorus
of joyful exultation!
A soft and gentle voice,
she called to me.
I reached out my trembling hand;
like lightning strikes
of untold storms
she touched me;
a soft and gentle hand
firmly grasping mine,
beckoning me forth.

I could not see
the shape or form
of her who spoke to me,
or whither she would lead,
but soon found myself
in glorious fields
of thick pastures green,
windswept forests tall,
where moss grew thick
and flowers bloomed.
Air filled
with sweetest fragrance.

She bid me lie there
in the glowing of her light,

and then I finally saw her.
The face of she
who spoke to me;
so beautiful it was,
I thought perhaps
this was but a dream,
but once again
she spoke to me
in joyful, soulful voice,
and grasped my trembling hands
in hers.
Dark, her hair,
with red locks
falling down about her
slender shoulders;
eyes, like doves,
so pure.
Her soft silken skin,
such perfect texture
wonderful to touch.
Her full, supple breasts,
like fawns joyful,
jumping in the fields
ready for play;
lips, like scarlet ribbons
on a mouth so lovely,
her face so blissful to behold!

"Come, my lover, come,
your winter night is done;
rains are gone,
summer is upon us!
The rejoicing songs of
birds fill the air,
and I will ravish you,
my lover; I will shelter
you in my love."

Her lips
tasted of dripping honeycomb,
milk and honey flowing
from her tongue.
Crimson upon her breasts;
a garden fountain of delight;
her senses filling my days
consuming my nights;
dreams of my sleep.
Fragrances of her love,
overwhelming.
She was radiant in her beauty
and I wept at the sight
of her;
lost, I was
at the touch of her.
The cheeks that surrounded
that magic place of her love
were beds of spices
and a feast of infinite delight.

She bid me love her there
beneath the ancient trees;
beside the rippling brook
on a bed of moss;
my love as strong
as death itself,
burning like a blazing fire
that will not be quenched.
We sang of our love there
And, when love was spent,
of joys yet still to come.

Somehow, then when I awoke,
the light and sounds of her song
I carry with me,
no shadow following.
I hear her calling to me

every day.
I lose myself
in the light of my lover;
she,
sun of my day,
brightest star of my night;
dawn that fills my sky.
All darkness is gone.

Oh, You!

Light like rain
washed over us;
I don't care where we are.

Night comes upon us,
the moon in tow;
we chased stars.

Water was our playground;
so many places
on a single breath.

I chased your shadow,
or was it my dream?
They are the same.

Time is a measure;
we don't even know
when we are.

Oh, you!
You are the best of my days;
I want to fly higher than now.

Where Are the Words?

It has been said, so I heard
a picture paints a thousand words.
There are not enough words
to paint the picture I have of you.

Oh, where? Where are the words
when my heart is so full?
Images of you burned in my mind.
Words! Words so hard to find.

Lost in your eyes, adrift in a dream
where perfect light shines, it seems,
on your angelic face—a thousand words?
Nay! a million words would ne'er suffice.

I draw you closely to my breast;
my heart trembles, I touch your face,
caressing and gently kissing you.
Come! Come, my love, let me be your rest.

Oh, the anguish! The torment!
Where are words when the heart is so full?
Torn between the love I know
and words I just can't seem to let flow.

What words will you give me?
Do you see what I see?
Images of you seared into my soul.
Oh, where are words when my heart is so full?

Mere words could never measure the pain
I feel, when tears fill your eyes.
What words could I e'er conceive
to plumb the depths of your soul?

Oh, no! My love! Words could surely never
know the agony of such loss
I would feel should you sever
the love I know for you.

So all these things I know so real.
Words can never paint what I feel.
Words! Oh, where are the words
when my heart is so full?

11

Faith

This is the place where everything that has gone before comes together in one big messy pile, and somehow finally makes sense to me, even when it defies all human logic and understanding. In the end, I really do believe in angels. Somehow, looking back, I see they've been there all along.

If Ever, Lord

Anger,
a tumultuous sea;
towering, cresting wave,
it crashes all around me.
I cannot see the dawning light
through the darkness of my life's fury.

Anger
in my soul
clouds my mind;
doubt and curses are all I find.
But if ever, Lord, I needed you,
I know I need you now.

Lord,
I weary so of this darkness;
but what then would I do,
should I call and not find you there?
After all I have said and done,
you would have the right not to care.

Psalm of a Summer Eve

The water
       still
mirrors the color
orange,
glowing sunset
         calm
waves lap
against the
sandy shore.
Fish
swim
gaily about
in their world,
         cool summer night
this reality
broken here
and there
by man's efforts,
         marred by sin,
greed;
earth's beauty
fading
away
like the setting sun;
things are turning
dark.

Whose World?

This is the junkie's world,
and my listening ears,
hear the screams that round me ring;
the music of the spheres.

This is the killer's world:
these men their rifles raise,
to kill the right and smash the light,
fulfill their leader's cravings.

This is the army's world:
they shine when e'er they kill.
They hide in the grass; they hear the foe pass,
and shoot him till he's still.

This is the devil's world,
O let me ne'er forget.
The evil light, the monster might,
deceives all over the world.

To Follow Or to Lead

I have got to keep my head up,
got to take a stand.
I have got to show the world
they are dealing with a man.

Must I stand alone?
For what then shall I stand?
Who will follow if I lead?
If I raise a banner, who will heed?

Are there not enough that stand?
Enough that stand alone?
Enough that know not where they go
or who and whither to they lead?

"Lead on, man," no, "Follow;" hear the cry!
But all are we together, on life's lonely road.
In the end we all must die,
whether on a pony or a stallion we rode.

Leave behind our mark, we must;
what are we, creatures of the dust?
The world treads on the long road ahead,
and leaves behind its memory of the dead.

When my soul, before God, stands,
what shall I say to Him who created man?
When before God's throne I pass,
where shall I be among the souls who died?

Follow whom? Oh, lead who where . . .?
Oh, no! For when I reach the High Place there,
then will I know whom I followed and whom I led.
Even now, I hear the screams of souls in Hell.

A Prayer

Lord, if you are really there,
and Lord, if you really care:
take all my tomorrows,
take away my sorrows
of today;
show me a better way.

It is hard to find true meaning
when life seems so demeaning;
when all around me
everywhere, I see lonely,
crying eyes.
Oh, Lord—why?
The hurting and the pain!
Fill me again,
help me rise above it all.
Lord, let me hear the call.
Dry my tears,
take away my fears . . .

Lord, if you're really there
and Lord, if you really care,
take all my tomorrows,
take away my sorrows
of today;
show me a better way.

An Easter Mystery

No faith, though great,
could move thee.
No eloquence, though moving,
would compel thee.
No prayer, though earnest,
no desire, though intense,
could avail thee.
No power, so awesome,
no might, so invincible,
could cause thee to tremble.
No riches
to entice thee;
no beauty
to seduce thee;
no government
to rule thee.

Thy love!
It was thy love
that hung thee there,
helpless and immovable.

Thy mercy!
It was thy mercy
that brought thee down to man,
the eternal in the flesh.

Thy compassion,
oh! thy great compassion!
But what mockery in return!

The crown of thorns,
blood run down,
beatings and the pain,
insults and the mockery,

spitting and the shame;
the cross thee had to carry.

Thy friends who all forsook thee;
only enemies to own thee.
Thy enemies who killed thee!

I wondered
as I read on,
why wouldst thou endure it all?

My anger was aroused.
"Destroy the enemy," I cried,

until I saw,
yes, until I saw
that though I thought
I would have been
that valiant friend,
thy friends had all left thee
in the end.
So I could not,
I could not say
I would have been that friend,
for no friend was represented there.

Thy enemies!
Thy enemies surrounded thee.
I wondered greatly at the cry,
"Father, forgive them,
for they know not what they do."

Then it struck me like a blazing, searing light;
thou cried that prayer for me!
It was I!
It was I that hung thee there!
I was that enemy;

I mocked thee,
I struck thee,
I cursed thee,
I spat on thee,
and it was I, finally,
who crucified thee.

It was for me,
the enemy,
thy sworn and bitter enemy,
that thou prayed.

I stood there smitten and broken,
humbled,
ashamed,
astonished,
and amazed,

for still greater now the mystery,
as I watched on in great perplexity.
It was thine own will
that this should happen to thee;
to take the sins I committed
with thee to the tree.
For thou knew it well beforehand:
I could never pay the penalty
I inflicted on thee.

As I stood
before the cross in shame,
I heard thee once again
softly,
it was but a whisper,
but I heard it plain:
"Father, forgive him,
forgive him also for his sin."

The fire burned hot within my soul
as I hear thee cry,
"My God, my God,
why hast thou forsaken Me?"

For as I stood before the cross,
it suddenly occurred to me
it was I,
it was I who justly deserved
to be forsaken.

I sank down trembling
slowly to my knees,
and once again I hear him call me.
I look up at him in great despair;
upon him whom I had struck,
upon whom I had spit,
whom I had cursed,
whom I had mocked and insulted,
at whom I had laughed in scorn,
and finally crucified.

For now the greatest mystery of all I see,
as he looked down and spoke to me.
"Verily," he said, "verily I say to thee,
thou also shalt with me in Paradise be."

To Mom and Dad

It has been a long, long time
since I told you
I love you.
I do
truly love you.

It has been even longer
since I told you
I am sorry.
And I am.
You gave me your all;
I always made you sad.

And now, before you go,
I want you to know
I will see you in heaven.
And I will.
Yes, in heaven.

You are on in years,
and my eyes fill with tears
at the thought of seeing you go.
I want you to know
I will see you in heaven.
Yes, in heaven.

I do not know the color of your eyes.
It makes me cry to realize
I never looked
or saw the love you had for me.

It is something I could never admit,
but as I grow old,
I love you more and more.
And I want you to know,

as you grow old,
I think of you every day.
And I do.

In this world of tears and deep despair,
your love has helped me through
my darkest hours;
though it has often seemed to me
love is nothing more than
a pile of twisted, broken dreams.

When you finally reach the end
of your life's journey,
do not be afraid for me.
My love
will be buried with you forever,
and I will see you in heaven.
Yes, in heaven.

Song for Satan

Oh, how I hate
what you have done to me!
The things you made me believe!
You made me so blind
I could not see
the lies;
I did not even know
they lived
inside of me.

You robbed me blind
and left me with nothing
but my life.
You stripped me naked,
you left me bare;
then you laughed at me
and left me standing there.
I hate you so much!
I choke on my words!
I cried out for love,
I cried, I cried, I cried,
but you never heard.
I needed love!
I turned to you,
I worshipped you,
but you just used me,
spat me out
and left me to die.
You gave me music and movies,
you showed me how to dance.
You gave me clothes and cars,
you even gave me romance.

But when it all was over
you never gave me so much as a glance.
I was lost and all alone.
You left me with just my soul,
and now you want that too.
But I have got some news.
Have I got some news for you!
I will never give that to you.
No! No! No!
You will never have the pleasure
of watching me die for you.

Finally,
when I could not
take it anymore,
it was then that I saw Jesus
come walking through the door.
He picked up my broken spirit,
up from off the floor,
and told me that he understood
because he, too,
had been down that road before.
He was the Son of God,
had endless love to give;
but you hated him so much,
you could not let him live.
You whipped and stripped him naked,
you beat him till he died.
He cried out and was forsaken
by his own Father,
God on High.
He walked down that road

for me,
so I don't have to die.
Now, Satan,
you can't deceive me
with your cursed lies.
Once I was yours,
but just as you thought
you had Jesus before
(you know you never really had him),
now you don't have me,
anymore.